MW01054791

Santa Fe Memories

Betty Carlson

Santa Fe Memories

Written and Compiled by Richard Mahler

Artwork by Betty Carlson

TRAVEL MEMORIES PRESS

Indianapolis • Toronto

Santa Fe Memories
First Edition

Text © 2002 by Richard Mahler
Artwork © 2002 by Betty Carlson

ISBN 0-89730-241-9

Publisher: R. J. Berg
Series Editor: Ginny Berg

TRAVEL MEMORIES PRESS
P. O. Box 30225
Indianapolis, IN 46230-0225
Phone 317.251.4640 or 800.638.3909
E-mail r.j.berg@worldnet.att.net

Printed in Italy

Front cover illustration: Santuario de Guadalupe Tower
Back cover illustration: Garden Path

Contents

Illustrations

Acknowledgments

Café Pasqual's –
   Owner/Executive Chef
   Katharine Kagel

Café San Estévan –
   Owner/Chef Estévan García

Corn Dance Café –
   Owner/Executive Chef
   Loretta Barrett Oden

Coyote Café –
   Owner/Executive Chef
   Mark Miller; Chef Scott Newman;
   Head Line Chef Ben Hargett

Fuego at La Posada –
   Chef Gary Palm

Gabriel's –
   Chef Saul Padilla

Guadalupe Café –
   Owner/Chef Isabelle Koomoa

La Casa Sena –
   Executive Chef Kelly Rogers

La Plazuela Restaurant at La Fonda
   Hotel – Executive Chef Lane Warner;
   Food Services Director Bert Leyva

María's New Mexican Kitchen –
   Owner/Executive Chef Al Lucero

The Mine Shaft Tavern –
   Owner Ede Salkeld-Cato

The Old House at Hotel Eldorado –
   Executive Chef Martín Ríos;
   Public Relations Director Jennifer Ríos

Paul's Restaurant –
  Owner/Executive Chef Paul Hunsicker

The Pink Adobe –
  Chef Mike Roybal; Co-owner/
  General Manager Joe Hoback

Restaurante Rancho de Chimayó –
  Chef Janet Malcom;
  Manager Mary Cordes

SantaCafé –
  Chef David Sellers;
  Manager Jill Cashman;
  Co-owner Bobby Morean

The Shed and La Choza –
  Co-owner Courtney Carswell

At the Santa Fe Convention & Visitors
  Bureau – Steve Lewis, Public Relations
  Consultant

And, special thanks to Nicky Leach for
  editorial assistance.

Introduction

Santa Fe proudly wears the title The City Different, and for good reason—the differences that characterize New Mexico's capital city run the gamut from its distinctive earth-tone architecture to its chile-flavored cuisine.

Santa Fe's unique appearance draws heavily on the city's long tenure as Spain's northernmost colonial capital in the New World and its earlier incarnation as a Native American village. Walls of buildings are thick and traditionally made of adobe bricks. Flat roofs are held up by beams made of the long trunks of ponderosa pines. The oldest structures have gently curved forms, tiny windows, and floors made of hard-packed mud.

Hailed as one of the world's most cosmopolitan and arts-oriented small cities, Santa Fe has been a crossroads of commerce and culture for centuries. Indians from the mountains traded here with their counterparts from the plains. Throughout most of the early 1800s, the Santa Fe Trail brought East Coast goods to what was then part of Mexico. As a United States territory, New Mexico fused traditions forged by American cowboys, Hispanic farmers, and Native American hunters.

Artists and writers followed in the twentieth century, inspired by Santa Fe's tolerance for diversity and its striking natural beauty. By the end of that century, the city was widely known for its art fairs, theater companies, symphony orchestra, outdoor summer opera, and chamber music festival. Musicians, filmmakers, poets, actors, painters, sculptors, and authors share both their creativity and their lives here. Others have come because of the opportunities for skiing, hiking, fishing, boating, and horseback riding, or to visit nearby Indian pueblos and national monuments.

Santa Fe is home to New Mexico's state capitol and government offices, but it is perhaps best known for its museums, restaurants, gift shops, and nearly two hundred art galleries. Among the city's seventy thousand residents is an unusually large number of movie stars, New Age healers, nuclear physicists, retired millionaires, and massage therapists—and a plethora of waiters and waitresses with college degrees.

At an elevation of seven thousand feet, Santa Fe is blessed with a relatively mild climate. The sun shines more than three hundred days each year. Summers are marked by warm days and crisp nights, with occasional thunderstorms and incredible displays of lightning. Winter is cool and bright, with modest snowfalls that melt quickly. Spring is a riot of blossoming fruit trees, while autumn is perhaps the best season of all, with leaves turning every imaginable shade of red, yellow, and orange.

In Santa Fe, you should expect the unexpected: A coyote's howl rouses you before dawn, an Asian chef's New Mexican tamales delight you at noon, and a stunning light show above the Jémez Mountains leaves you breathless at sunset. Those who know it well say the best way to experience Santa Fe is simply to give in to the refreshing ambience of one of the world's most distinctive cities—one that nurtures travelers, always encouraging them to look at things in a new way.

British novelist D. H. Lawrence may have said it best after his first visit: "The moment I saw the brilliant, proud morning sun shine high up over the desert of Santa Fe, something stood still in my soul."

Santa Fe's Multicultural History

Thousands of years ago, Indians farmed and hunted in the area that would become Santa Fe. They built a pueblo (settlement) here as early as the 1300s. The first Europeans to visit the vicinity of present-day Santa Fe were Spanish explorers who passed through in the mid-sixteenth century in their quest for gold. Spanish colonists settled nearby in 1598, and La Villa Real de la Santa Fé (The Royal City of the Holy Faith) was formally founded in 1610 and named capital of Spain's New Mexico territory.

The well-organized Pueblo Indian Revolt of 1680—a response to slavery and mistreatment—resulted in Spain's withdrawal from New Mexico until 1692. Spain eventually reasserted its control over Santa Fe, and relations among the Spanish and

Pueblo peoples improved dramatically. During the 1700s, more Spanish colonists poured into the region and set up farms and established villages near the thriving capital, while Native Americans were generally allowed to retain their land and other property.

Santa Fe became part of the Republic of Mexico in 1821, after Spain relinquished most of its New World colonies. Mexican rule did not last long, though, as the region came under the jurisdiction of the United States at the beginning of the Mexican War in 1846. The new, more open political climate resulted in an influx of goods and immigrants from the east, which quickly transformed Santa Fe from a sleepy, Spanish-speaking outpost to a lively trade center on the fast-growing American frontier. New Mexico was granted statehood in 1912, with the capital remaining in Santa Fe.

NATIVE AMERICANA

CORN DANCE CAFÉ

Loretta Barrett Oden began her love affair with food while growing up on the Citizen Potawatomi Indian reservation in Shawnee, Oklahoma. Conscious of the powerful cultural bond between Native Americans and their food, Oden founded the Corn Dance Café in the early 1990s, using recipes representing more than a dozen tribes. The original Corn Dance was located in an old house on Water Street but has since moved to the Hotel Santa Fe, owned by the people of Picuris Pueblo. The Corn Dance's dishes feature traditional ingredients such as corn, tomatoes, chile, venison, bison, salmon, trout, elk, beans, cranberries, piñon nuts, sage, juniper berries, hickory nuts, acorns, and squash—all used by Native American cooks long before Europeans arrived in North America.

Roasted Bell Pepper and Piñon Nut Salad

PREHEAT OVEN to 400°F.

Combine all bell pepper halves in a large bowl; pour ½ cup oil over peppers and toss to coat. Place peppers, cut side down, on two or three baking sheets or jelly roll pans (be sure to use pans with sides to collect the juices). Sprinkle lightly and evenly with salt. Roast at 400°F for 20 to 30 minutes or until peppers are soft and skins are slightly blackened. Rearrange baking sheets in oven during roasting, if necessary, so all peppers are evenly roasted and blackened.

Remove from oven and place peppers in large plastic bags, or leave peppers on baking sheets and cover with plastic wrap. Peppers will "sweat" as they cool. When peppers are cool enough to handle, peel and cut into ¼-inch strips. In a large bowl, combine pepper strips and juices, remaining 1½ tablespoons olive oil, and vinegar; toss lightly to coat. Cover and refrigerate or let stand at room temperature for at least 1 hour.

When ready to serve, drain peppers and transfer to a serving platter or bowl; discard marinade. Season with additional salt, if needed, and pepper flakes; sprinkle with piñon nuts.

Yield: 8 servings

2 large orange bell peppers, halved and seeded

2 large purple bell peppers, halved and seeded

2 large red bell peppers, halved and seeded

2 large yellow bell peppers, halved and seeded

½ cup plus 1½ tablespoons extra virgin olive oil, divided

Salt

1½ tablespoons (or more to taste) balsamic vinegar

Red pepper or chipotle pepper flakes

¼ cup roasted unsalted piñon nuts (pignolias or other pine nuts may be substituted; see Note)

Serving Note: Serve chilled or at room temperature. The salad may be prepared a day in advance and stored in the refrigerator.

Note: To dry-roast raw shelled piñon nuts, place nuts in a heavy skillet and cook over low heat, stirring frequently, for several minutes or until nuts are fragrant and light golden brown. Or, spread nuts on a baking sheet and bake at 350°F for 5 to 10 minutes, stirring often. Either way, watch carefully so nuts don't burn—their high oil content makes them brown quickly.

ON THE PLAZA

LA PLAZUELA RESTAURANT AT LA FONDA HOTEL

In Spanish, La Fonda means "the inn," and in Santa Fe, it also refers to what is perhaps the city's most famous hotel. The southeast corner of the Plaza—and the terminus of the famous Santa Fe Trail from Franklin, Missouri—has been the site of a lodging establishment since at least 1821 and probably as early as 1610. Merchants, trappers, outlaws, traders, entertainers, generals, and politicians (including Presidents Hayes and Grant) all passed through the doors of La Fonda's predecessors, which housed saloons, casinos, and a dining hall. The current hotel was built in Spanish-Pueblo Revival style in 1920, and its restaurant, La Plazuela, occupies an interior courtyard (the name means "little plaza") that was once open to the sky but is now covered with opaque glass to create an atrium.

Ceviche de Huachinango

2 fresh, skinless red snapper fillets
(about 8 ounces each), cut into ½-inch cubes

1 cup fresh lime juice

4 small Roma tomatoes, peeled, seeded,
and diced

1 large avocado, peeled, pitted, and diced

1 small red onion, peeled and diced

1 serrano chile pepper, seeded and minced

2 tablespoons chopped green olives

1½ tablespoons chopped fresh cilantro

1 teaspoon sugar

For garnish: fresh cilantro, chopped avocado,
slices of fresh lime

Tortilla chips or saltines

COMBINE FISH AND LIME JUICE in a glass bowl.
Cover and refrigerate for about 4 hours or until the
fish is thoroughly "cooked" by acidic reaction with
the juice. (The fish will become opaque when it is
ready.) Drain fish and discard lime juice. Rinse fish
lightly with water and drain again.

In a glass bowl, combine fish, tomatoes, avocado,
onion, chile pepper, olives, cilantro, and sugar; mix
gently. Cover and refrigerate for at least 30 minutes.

To serve, spoon ceviche into sundae glasses and
garnish with fresh cilantro, chopped avocado, and
slices of fresh lime. Serve with tortilla chips or
saltines.

Yield: 4 servings

PAST MEETS PRESENT
SantaCafé

SantaCafé occupies an 1857 adobe building that was constructed as the Territorial-style home of Padre José Manuel Gallegos. The flamboyantly controversial Gallegos was defrocked as a parish priest by the Catholic Church in 1851 for his alleged gambling, womanizing, dancing, and politicking. Ironically, he went on to become New Mexico Territory's sole delegate to the United States Congress in 1852. During the Civil War, the building was a rooming house, and it later became an Episcopalian chapel. When architect Jim Bibo opened SantaCafé here in 1983, he preserved the building's sense of timelessness: At one end of the reception area is an old water well that was once used by the Gallegos family but is now covered by Plexiglas. Meals are served in starkly minimalist all-white rooms and, during warm months, in a peaceful, boulder-strewn courtyard.

Crème Brûlée

1 quart heavy cream

¾ cup sugar

1 vanilla bean, split lengthwise

1 pint whole eggs
(about 10 to 12 medium eggs),
lightly beaten

Additional sugar for tops of desserts

For garnish: fresh berries

IN A LARGE SAUCEPAN, combine cream, sugar, and vanilla bean; bring slowly to a boil, stirring gently with a plastic spatula. Occasionally squeeze or agitate the vanilla bean to release its seeds. (Have ready a whisk, a strainer, and a three-quart container.) When the cream mixture reaches its boiling point, pour in the eggs while whisking vigorously. Once all is well blended and cooled by the eggs, stir more gently. In a few minutes, the mixture will begin to thicken as it reaches the boiling point again. When mixture resembles the texture of yogurt, remove from heat while whisking steadily. This allows the mixture to cool and aerate. Strain into the container, then smooth out any grainy parts with a hand blender. Pour into custard cups or small bowls and refrigerate for at least 4 hours, uncovered.

Spread a small amount of granulated sugar on top of each dessert. Caramelize with a kitchen blowtorch or by placing under the broiler, rotating the containers as this is being done. Serve right away. Fresh berries are an appropriate accompaniment.

Yield: 8 to 10 servings

STAAB'S HAUNTED MANSION

FUEGO AT LA POSADA

Today it is an upscale hotel and spa, but La Posada grew from humble origins. During most of the nineteenth century, this property was part of a farm owned by the Baca family. In 1876, wealthy merchant Abraham Staab bought a parcel of the land, where he later built a three-story brick mansion. His wife, Julia, suffered from severe depression and died in 1896 in an upstairs bedroom. A ghost resembling Julia Staab is said to have roamed the building ever since and remains a familiar sight to hotel employees. Guests occasionally see her in the bar and adjacent Victorian sitting rooms. The Staab family eventually sold the property and it became one of Santa Fe's most favored hotels. After extensive renovations in the late 1990s, the current owners rechristened their restaurant Fuego, Spanish for "fire."

8 ounces chicken breast

1½ teaspoons unsalted butter

1½ teaspoons olive oil

1 large yellow onion, diced

3 cups diced fresh tomatoes or 1 large can
(26 ounces) tomatoes, diced

1 jalapeño or serrano chile pepper, diced

¾ cup V-8 juice or other vegetable juice

2 cups hot water

2 tablespoons concentrated chicken base

1½ tablespoons tomato paste

¾ teaspoon chile powder

¾ teaspoon cumin

¾ teaspoon chopped fresh oregano

¾ teaspoon paprika

½ teaspoon finely chopped fresh garlic

½ teaspoon white pepper

2 tablespoons cornstarch

2 cups oil (for deep-frying)

6 fresh corn tortillas, cut into strips

1 avocado, peeled, pitted, and diced

2 tablespoons chopped fresh cilantro

For garnish: grated Asiago cheese

Tortilla Soup

GRILL CHICKEN BREAST, then cut into strips. Set aside.

Heat butter and olive oil in a large, heavy saucepan until butter melts. Add onion and cook over medium heat for about 5 minutes or until onion is translucent. Add tomatoes and cook for 5 minutes. Add chile pepper, V-8 or vegetable juice, and hot water; bring to a boil. Reduce heat to a medium simmer. Add chicken base, tomato paste, chile powder, cumin, oregano, paprika, garlic, and white pepper; cook, stirring occasionally, for 30 minutes. In a small bowl or cup, combine cornstarch with a little cold water and mix until smooth. Stir cornstarch into soup and continue cooking for about 10 minutes or until soup thickens.

Heat oil for deep-frying in a skillet. Add tortilla strips and fry until golden brown, about 1 to 2 minutes. Remove tortilla strips with a slotted spoon and drain on paper towels.

To serve, place equal amounts of chicken, fried tortilla strips, avocado, and cilantro in soup bowls—reserving some of these ingredients to use as garnishes, if desired. Ladle soup over ingredients in bowls. Add garnishes and serve with grated cheese.

Yield: 4 to 6 servings

FOOD FOR THE SOUL

CAFÉ SAN ESTÉVAN

By authority of the King of Spain, El Camino Real was once the "royal road" to transport people, livestock, and trade goods between Mexico City and Santa Fe. Today Agua Fría Street follows the northern end of El Camino Real, and at its terminus is Santuario de Guadalupe, which was sanctified in 1796 and is the oldest shrine to the Virgin of Guadalupe in the United States. Across the street is Estévan García's Café San Estévan. García learned the culinary arts as a child watching his mother cook. During the several years he spent as a Franciscan monk, he found cooking for his fellow friars "spiritually enlightening." García claims that the angels have inspired him to "elevate these beans and chiles to a new cuisine based on traditional northern New Mexico cooking methods."

Mushroom Filling

½ cup (1 stick) butter

16 fresh mushroom caps

1 cup cream

½ teaspoon salt

½ teaspoon pepper

Chile Sauce

1 cup veal stock

*½ cup red chile sauce
(prepared or homemade; see Note)*

Rellenos

*6 fresh green Anaheim chile peppers,
roasted, skinned, and seeded
(cut along one side to remove seeds)*

½ teaspoon salt

Green Chile Rellenos with Mushroom Filling

TO PREPARE MUSHROOM FILLING: Melt butter in a large saucepan over moderate heat. Add mushroom caps and sauté, stirring occasionally, until all liquid evaporates. Add cream, salt, and pepper; continue cooking, stirring occasionally, until mushrooms have absorbed most of the cream and the sauce is thick. Remove from heat and cool. Purée in blender.

TO PREPARE CHILE SAUCE: Combine veal stock and red chile sauce in a saucepan; cook over low heat until mixture thickens slightly. Remove from heat and keep warm.

TO PREPARE RELLENOS: Preheat oven to 425°F. Grease a baking sheet. Spread chiles open and sprinkle insides lightly with salt. Spoon 3 tablespoons Mushroom Filling into each chile, then close chiles around the filling. Place chiles, seam side down, on prepared baking sheet, cover with a damp towel, and bake at 425°F for about 10 minutes or until heated through.

To serve, spoon a small amount of Chile Sauce on each plate, then place Relleno on sauce.

Yield: 6 servings

Note: A simple red chile sauce can be made by puréeing the following ingredients in a blender: 12 fresh red chile peppers, roasted, peeled, stemmed, and seeded; 2 garlic cloves; ½ teaspoon dried oregano (preferably Mexican); ½ teaspoon salt; and 2 cups water.

Treasures of Art and Architecture

A new wave of outsiders began transforming the look and feel of Santa Fe in the 1920s and 1930s. Legendary figures in the arts who spent time here include painter Georgia O'Keeffe, writer D. H. Lawrence, poet Witter Bynner, photographer Ansel Adams, and novelist Willa Cather. This informal and ever-changing art colony has swelled to include hundreds of creative individuals today.

The simultaneous revival of Spanish Colonial and Native American arts and crafts traditions helped put Santa Fe on the map as a favored tourist destination. Native American artists continue to offer fine jewelry, pottery, carvings, and sand paintings beneath the portal of the Palace of the Governors, and descendants of New Mexico's original Spanish settlers offer religious-themed paintings and wood carvings, pressed tinwork, furniture, weavings, and embroidery.

Although Santa Fe's distinctive architecture has been around for much longer, it wasn't until early in the twentieth century that the city's residents began preserving and promoting what eventually became known as Santa Fe style. The elements of this look include mud-plastered adobe-brick walls and flat roofs supported by peeled pine beams. These are essentially the same building techniques used by the Pueblo Indians who lived in the area before Europeans arrived, with modifications such as glass windows and roof parapets added by Spanish colonists. The Territorial style was, as the name implies, introduced between 1846 and 1912, when New Mexico was under U.S. control but not a state. Among other elements, it is marked by brickwork along the tops of exterior walls and milled woodwork around windows.

A Family Legacy

The Pink Adobe

Santa Fe is a small city, but not long ago it was considerably smaller—the sort of lazy, relaxed place where you would always see someone you knew while out on an errand. The few bars and restaurants that existed were usually run by long-time residents and their family members. One of the last vestiges of this tradition is The Pink Adobe, founded in 1945 by painter Rosalea Murphy in an Old Santa Fe Trail building that was once a barracks for Spanish soldiers. Murphy could often be found in The Dragon Room, the friendly bar (with a tree growing through the roof!) that she opened in 1978 at the entrance of "The Pink." Murphy's family continues to run the restaurant, using many of the original recipes Rosalea developed over the years.

Steak Dunigan

TO PREPARE PINK ADOBE GREEN CHILE: In a large pot, combine chiles, tomatoes, salt, cilantro, garlic powder, oregano, and cumin; mix well. Place pot over low heat. In a separate pan, lightly sauté onion in butter. Add sautéed onion to chile mixture; simmer for about 20 minutes, stirring occasionally.

TO PREPARE STEAKS AND MUSHROOMS: Sprinkle Char Crust Rub or hickory smoke salt on both sides of steaks. Broil or grill to desired doneness (about 10 minutes for rare, 15 minutes for medium), turning once. While steaks are cooking, sauté mushrooms in butter for about 5 minutes or until soft. Drizzle lemon juice over mushrooms. Remove from heat and keep warm.

To serve, place a steak on each plate and top with mushrooms, then cover with green chile.

Yield: 6 servings

Pink Adobe Green Chile

2 cups mild green chile (frozen)

1 cup hot green chile (frozen)

½ cup canned whole tomatoes, squished

1½ teaspoons salt

¼ teaspoon dried cilantro

¼ teaspoon garlic powder

¼ teaspoon dried oregano

⅛ teaspoon ground cumin

1 large onion, chopped

¼ cup (½ stick) butter

Steaks and Mushrooms

Char Crust Rub or hickory smoke salt

6 top-grade New York sirloin steaks (14 to 16 ounces each)

12 large mushrooms, sliced

¼ cup (½ stick) butter

Juice of ½ lemon (about 1½ tablespoons)

A House of History

La Casa Sena

La Casa Sena restaurant occupies a nineteenth-century adobe mansion with a colorful history. In the 1830s, José and Ysabel Sena started living in a small adobe house on this spot. During the 1860s, the Senas expanded their home to thirty-three rooms that accommodated the family—including their eleven children—and various servants, horses, and chickens. A ballroom on the second floor was used for courtship balls in honor of the Sena daughters, and temporarily housed the territorial legislature after a fire burned the state capitol. During the early 1940s, the headquarters of the top secret Manhattan Project, undertaken in nearby Los Alamos, was based here. Today the dining room at La Casa Sena is decorated with museum-quality art, and the tree-shaded interior courtyard of Sena Plaza (once the feeding ground for goats) offers outdoor dining in warm weather.

Trout in Adobe

PLACE CORN HUSKS in a shallow pan; cover with water and set aside to soften.

Melt 2 tablespoons butter in a sauté pan. Add mushrooms and garlic; sauté for about 5 minutes or until soft. Increase heat and add wine and salt; cook 2 minutes longer. Remove from heat and cool slightly, then whisk in remaining butter. Set aside to cool (mixture will become firm as it cools).

Using a rolling pin, roll out each of the eight clay slabs to form a 12 x 18-inch rectangle that is ½ inch thick. Drain corn husks and shake off excess water.

Preheat oven to 400°F. Divide butter-mushroom mixture into four equal portions. Sandwich one portion of the mixture between two trout fillets, then wrap the fillets in two or three corn husks so the fish is completely covered. Place the husk-wrapped fish lengthwise on a rectangle of clay, then top with another rectangle of clay. Mold clay around fish and press edges of clay with the tines of a fork to seal. Cut small air vents in the top portion of clay so steam can escape during cooking. Repeat this process with remaining ingredients.

Place clay-encased trout on a sturdy cookie sheet or directly on an oven rack. Bake at 400°F for 15 to 20 minutes. The clay will become pale, dry, and hard during baking.

To serve, crack clay open (in the kitchen or at the table) with a large metal spoon. Remove husks from fish and discard husks. Place fish on a bed of assorted salad greens and garnish with lemon wedges.

Yield: 4 servings

Note: Low-fire clay can be purchased at art or hobby supply stores. Be sure the clay is nontoxic; otherwise, the food could become contaminated.

8 to 12 dried corn husks

1 cup (2 sticks) butter, softened and divided

2 cups sliced mushrooms

1 tablespoon minced fresh garlic

½ cup white wine

Salt

5 pounds nontoxic, low-fire clay, divided into eight 20-ounce slabs (see Note)

4 whole trout, filleted into eight pieces (skin and heads removed)

Assorted salad greens (arugula, romaine, or mixed lettuces)

For garnish: 4 lemon wedges

CORNER OF CONTENTMENT

CAFÉ PASQUAL'S

One day in 1978, a new arrival to Santa Fe walked into Theo Raven's Water Street gift shop, Doodlet's, and struck up a conversation. "See that restaurant across the street?" Theo eventually asked her new friend. "Go buy it!" And the rest, as they say, is history. Former Chinese food caterer Katharine Kagel soon transformed the old Pueblo-style building—once a Texaco gas station—into Café Pasqual's, named after the patron saint of Mexican and New Mexican kitchens and cooks. Besides regional dishes based on fresh, locally grown ingredients, Pasqual's serves meals influenced by Asia (where Kagel has lived) and Mexico (where she loves to travel). Her many humanitarian activities serve to confirm Kagel's motto, emblazoned on Café Pasqual's latté cups: "Panza llena, corazón contento (Full stomach, contented heart)!"

Huevos Motuleños

Green Chile Sauce

¾ pound (approximately) fresh green chile peppers (New Mexico or Anaheim), roasted and peeled

¼ cup diced white onion

2 garlic cloves, minced

⅔ teaspoon dried marjoram or Mexican oregano

1⅓ cups water

1½ tablespoons all-purpose flour

1 tablespoon vegetable oil

Salt

To Prepare Green Chile Sauce: Chop roasted chile peppers and measure 1 cup. In a saucepan, combine chile peppers, onion, garlic, and marjoram or oregano; add water and cook over medium heat for 5 minutes. Reduce heat and simmer, uncovered, for 20 to 30 minutes, stirring occasionally.

Combine flour and oil in a small saucepan; whisk until smooth and well blended. Cook over medium-high heat for about 1 minute or until mixture bubbles. Reduce heat to low and cook, whisking constantly, for 3 or 4 minutes or until mixture turns light brown. Gradually add chile mixture, whisking constantly until well blended. Continue cooking for about 15 minutes or until sauce thickens. Season with salt. Remove from heat and keep warm.

Salsa Fresca

5 plum tomatoes, diced

¼ cup (approximately) diced onion

*½ serrano or 1 jalapeño chile pepper,
stemmed, seeded, and minced*

¼ cup chopped fresh cilantro

Juice of 1 lime (about 1 to 2 tablespoons)

Salt

Veggies, Eggs, Etc.

*2 cups cooked black beans
(homemade or canned)*

1 cup shelled green peas (fresh or frozen)

*8 corn tortillas
(use blue tortillas, if available)*

3 or 4 tablespoons vegetable oil

*¼ cup plus 2 tablespoons clarified butter,
divided*

4 bananas, peeled and cut in half lengthwise

8 eggs

4 cups Green Chile Sauce

1 cup feta cheese, crumbled

1⅓ cups Salsa Fresca

For garnish: 8 sprigs fresh cilantro

TO PREPARE SALSA FRESCA: In a small bowl, combine tomatoes, onion, chile pepper, cilantro, and lime juice, adjusting quantities of onion and chile to your taste; stir to mix. Season with salt. Set aside.

TO PREPARE VEGGIES, EGGS, ETC.: Heat beans, then remove from heat and keep warm. Cook peas in boiling water for 1 or 2 minutes or just until tender, then drain and keep warm. Brush tortillas with oil, then cook— one at a time—in a dry skillet over high heat for about 5 seconds per side, turning once. Set aside and keep warm. Melt ¼ cup clarified butter in a sauté pan over medium heat; when butter sizzles, add bananas and cook for about 5 minutes on each side or until golden brown. In another sauté pan, melt remaining 2 tablespoons clarified butter over medium heat. Add eggs and cook as desired (fried or scrambled).

TO ASSEMBLE HUEVOS MOTULEÑOS: Place two tortillas side by side on each plate. For each serving, spoon ½ cup beans over tortillas. Place cooked eggs on top of beans. Ladle Green Chile Sauce over eggs. Sprinkle with ¼ cup feta cheese and ¼ cup peas. Top with ⅓ cup Salsa Fresca and place two fried banana halves on the side of the plate. Garnish with cilantro sprigs and serve immediately.

Yield: 4 servings

An Adobe Treasure

The Old House at Hotel Eldorado

The largest hotel (and building) in downtown Santa Fe, Hotel Eldorado was built in 1986 in Spanish-Pueblo Revival style. Although the hotel has become a highly respected part of the community, there was considerable local opposition to the Eldorado at the time of its construction, in part because its developers planned to demolish a nineteenth-century adobe home that stood near the center of the proposed project. The structure was spared, however, and became—in remodeled form—The Old House restaurant, now completely surrounded by (and incorporated within) the hotel, but retaining its Territorial-era ambience. Mexico-born executive chef Martín Ríos oversees the restaurant's "contemporary global cuisine," which, he says, utilizes Southwestern ingredients and many other specialized flavorings from India, Mexico, and East Asia, as well as French techniques.

Savory Pan-Roasted Lump Crab Cakes with Papaya Cilantro Salsa and Smoked Tomatillo Jalapeño Vinaigrette

TO PREPARE PAPAYA CILANTRO SALSA: Combine all ingredients in a medium bowl and mix well. Cover and refrigerate until ready to serve.

TO PREPARE SMOKED TOMATILLO JALAPEÑO VINAIGRETTE: In blender container, combine all ingredients except walnut oil, salt, and pepper; process until mixture is smooth. Slowly add oil with blender running and process until well blended. Season with salt and pepper. Strain vinaigrette, then set aside.

Papaya Cilantro Salsa

1 ripe papaya, peeled and diced

2 tablespoons chopped tomatoes

1 tablespoon chopped fresh cilantro

1 tablespoon chopped red onion

1 tablespoon chile-flavored oil

1 teaspoon minced gingerroot

*Zest of ½ lemon, minced
(about 1 to 2 teaspoons)*

Salt and pepper

Smoked Tomatillo Jalapeño Vinaigrette

*1 pound tomatillos, lightly smoked
(see Note)*

*1 small jalapeño chile pepper, stemmed,
seeded, and finely minced*

3 tablespoons chopped fresh cilantro

2 tablespoons chopped fresh parsley

1 garlic clove, minced

1 tablespoon honey

Juice of 1 lime (about 1 to 2 tablespoons)

1 cup clam juice

½ cup walnut oil

Salt and pepper

Crab Cakes

12 ounces lump crabmeat

*½ cup fresh breadcrumbs
(use more for drier crab cakes)*

½ cup mayonnaise

*4 tablespoons (¼ cup) grated
pepper jack cheese*

2 tablespoons minced red bell pepper

2 tablespoons minced yellow bell pepper

2 tablespoons minced celery

1 tablespoon minced red onion

1 tablespoon finely chopped fresh parsley

*1 tablespoon finely chopped
fresh tarragon*

1 tablespoon finely chopped fresh thyme

1 tablespoon Dijon mustard

1 tablespoon all-purpose flour

1 cup vegetable oil

*For garnish: daikon sprouts or
jicama slices (optional)*

TO PREPARE CRAB CAKES: In a medium bowl, combine all ingredients except flour and oil; mix well. Cover and refrigerate for 10 minutes. Divide crab mixture into four equal portions, then form each portion into a cake. Dust crab cakes lightly with flour. Heat oil in a sauté pan over medium heat. Sauté crab cakes for about 2 minutes per side or until both sides are crispy.

To serve, place one crab cake on each plate, then spoon salsa around crab cake. Drizzle with vinaigrette and garnish with daikon sprouts or jicama slices, if desired. Serve immediately.

Yield: 4 servings

Note: To smoke tomatillos in a home smoker, clean tomatillos and soak in cold water for about 3 minutes. Drain and place in a small aluminum pan. Place pan in hot smoker for 3 to 4 minutes. Remove from smoker and cool.

The Many Tastes of Santa Fe

The key ingredient in New Mexico's indigenous cuisine can be summed up in a single word: chile, spelled with an "e." In Santa Fe, as in the rest of the state, the use of spicy chile peppers is so common that the New Mexico legislature has designated an official state question—"Red or green?"—that refers to a diner's preference for red or green chile. (Red tends to be milder than green; ask for "Christmas" and you'll get some of each.) The chile has been the official "state vegetable" since 1965, though this member of the capsicum family is actually a fruit. Long strings of dried chiles, called *ristras*, hang within arm's reach in many New Mexican kitchens. They were once bartered like money and used to ward off witches.

Chile—not to be confused with chili, a chile pepper–flavored stew of meat and, sometimes, beans—makes an appearance of some kind in almost all classic New Mexican dishes, including *calabacitas* (a corn and squash casserole), *frijoles pintos* (boiled pinto beans), and *tamales* (corn flour dough wrapped around meat or vegetables and cooked in a corn husk).

New Mexico's traditional dishes are often similar to those found in Old Mexico, yet their differences reflect the region's strong Native American influences and its long period of isolation from the United States, Spain, and the interior of Mexico. Even the desserts have a unique flavor; favorites include *sopaipillas* (airy, deep-fried dough drizzled with honey), *bizcochitos* (anise-flavored sugar cookies), and piñon nut candy (chocolate fudge studded with locally gathered pine nuts).

FOR THE LOVE OF CHILE

GUADALUPE CAFÉ

anta Fe's central district is divided by the Santa Fe River, a tree-shaded stream that flows east to west through the city's center. The commercial and historic core lies on the north side of the river while most state government buildings, including the capitol, are on the south. Between the capitol and the river is the Barrio de Analco, an old neighborhood where you'll find San Miguel Chapel, built originally in 1626 and believed to be the city's oldest continuously used church; Santa Fe's oldest house (at 215 East de Vargas Street), said to date from the early 1600s; and the Guadalupe Café, situated in a tile-roofed house adjacent to the capitol on Old Santa Fe Trail.

Jalapeño Pepper Cheese Soup

IN A MEDIUM SAUCEPAN, combine broth, celery, tomatoes, onion, and oregano; bring to a boil. Reduce heat and simmer for 30 minutes.

In a food processor or blender, combine half of the vegetable-broth mixture with half of the cheese. Process until mixture is smooth, then transfer to a saucepan. Process remaining vegetable-broth mixture and cheese, then add to saucepan. Cook over low heat, stirring often, just until heated through. Ladle into soup bowls and garnish with chile peppers and cilantro.

Yield: 8 to 10 servings

6 cups unsalted chicken broth
4 stalks celery, diced
3 tomatoes, diced
1 medium onion, chopped
4 tablespoons dried Mexican oregano
5 pounds Velveeta cheese, cubed
6 fresh jalapeño chile peppers, finely diced
4 tablespoons chopped fresh cilantro

A Burro Alley Tradition
The Shed and La Choza

The Shed restaurant started out in 1953 on Burro Alley in what was, literally, a shed. The barnlike structure was where woodcutters would shelter their burros after selling loads of firewood to Santa Fe residents; then the woodcutters would frequently go around the corner to San Francisco Street and spend some of their newfound cash on a meal or a slug of Taos Lightning whiskey before heading back into the mountains. In 1960, the restaurant moved to a Palace Street building with adobe walls that are three feet thick. The Shed's sister restaurant, La Choza, occupies the former headquarters and bunkhouse for Mercer Ranch, where crops and livestock were raised along Santa Fe's main irrigation ditch, Acequia Madre, which still flows alongside the Alarid Street restaurant.

2 cups dried posole
(also called dried corn or
hominy; see Note)

1 pound lean pork shoulder

4 dried red chile pods

Juice of 1 lime
(about 1 to 2 tablespoons)

3 garlic cloves, chopped

¼ teaspoon dried oregano

Salt

Red Chile Posole
(Hominy Stew)

COMBINE DRIED POSOLE (uncooked) and 2 quarts water in a medium bowl; cover and let soak at room temperature for at least 6 hours or overnight. When ready to cook, drain posole; then rinse with water and drain again.

In a heavy soup pot or large saucepan, combine posole, pork shoulder, chile pods, and lime juice; add just enough water to cover. Bring to a boil, then reduce heat, cover pot, and simmer for about 3 hours or until posole "pops open." Check often during cooking, stirring and adding hot water as needed to keep ingredients covered with liquid.

Remove pork shoulder and shred meat. Return shredded pork to pot along with garlic, oregano, and salt. Cover pot and simmer 30 minutes longer.

Yield: 8 servings

Serving Note: Serve posole with tortillas and toppings such as grated cheese, chopped radishes, diced onions, or shredded lettuce. Fresh lime wedges are sometimes used as garnishes—then the juice is squeezed into the posole.

Note: Dried posole is widely available in New Mexico but may be difficult to find elsewhere. Canned hominy may be used in place of the dried posole; it will not need to be soaked before cooking.

SUMPTUOUS SANTA FE STYLE
COYOTE CAFÉ

One of the most famous among Santa Fe's two hundred restaurants, Coyote Café was founded in 1987 (at the renovated location of Santa Fe's old bus depot) by anthropologist-turned-chef Mark Miller. His vision calls for a different menu each day, recreating Southwestern and Latin American dishes—some of which predate the arrival of Europeans in the New World. The décor of the Coyote is as striking as the food: a surreal mix of colors, a desert mural, and carved wooden animals adorn the stairway and dining room. During summer months, the adjacent Coyote Cantina serves simpler—yet equally upscale—Southwestern cuisine in a lively open-air bar. The Cantina is one of the few restaurants in Santa Fe where you can watch the sun set while you eat.

2 poblano chile peppers

2 red bell peppers

¾ cup olive oil, divided

1 large white onion, diced

2 Japanese eggplants, diced

1 head fennel, diced

2 green zucchini, diced

2 yellow squash, diced

3 garlic cloves, chopped

3 Roma tomatoes, peeled, seeded, and diced

1 cup chicken stock

2 tablespoons butter

2 tablespoons chopped fresh epazote (or fresh tarragon or basil)

Salt and pepper

2 cups Panko breadcrumbs

5 tablespoons ground fresh horseradish

Zest of 4 lemons, finely chopped (about 2½ tablespoons)

⅛ cup (2 tablespoons) snipped chives

4 pieces halibut (6 ounces each)

Horseradish Crusted Halibut with Southwestern Ratatouille and Epazote

To Roast Peppers: Place poblanos and red bell peppers over an open flame. Burn the skin quickly (about 1½ minutes on each side) so as not to burn the flesh. Place roasted peppers in a bowl and cover with plastic wrap to steam. Wipe off burned skin and remove stems and seeds. Dice peppers, then set aside.

To Prepare Ratatouille: Heat ¼ cup olive oil in a large sauté pan. Add onion and eggplant; sauté for 2 minutes. Add fennel and cook for 1 minute. Add zucchini, yellow squash, garlic, and roasted peppers; cook for 2 minutes. Add tomatoes and chicken stock; cook for 1 minute. Finish with butter and epazote. Season to taste with salt and pepper.

To Prepare Halibut: Preheat oven to 375°F. In a mixing bowl, combine breadcrumbs, horseradish, lemon zest, chives, and ¼ cup olive oil; mix well, then set aside. Heat remaining ¼ cup olive oil in a sauté pan. Season halibut and sear in hot oil until golden, about 1½ to 2 minutes on each side. Place halibut on a buttered sheet pan and top with breadcrumb mixture. Bake at 375°F for about 3 minutes or until halibut is done.

To serve, spoon ratatouille in the center of each plate, then top with halibut.

Yield: 4 servings

Downtown Elegance

Paul's Restaurant

On one of Santa Fe's downtown side streets, a hole-in-the-wall restaurant provides a relaxed and intimate dining experience. Owner/executive chef Paul Hunsicker has been serving modern, international dishes here since 1990, combining fresh, delicious ingredients in an imaginative (and award-winning) way. The atmosphere is both upscale and casual, with eclectic folk art decorations that reflect Hunsicker's upbeat personality. Paul's Restaurant is situated in a modest building constructed during the 1940s, occupied over the years by a variety of retail stores and cafés. A few steps away is Santa Fe's federal courthouse, which has changed little since its completion in 1889. The oval street that curves around the courthouse is the last remnant of a racetrack for horses and burros that once circled the imposing stone building.

Salmon

8 ounces pecans, finely chopped

¼ cup (½ stick) butter, softened

1 tablespoon finely chopped fresh basil

1 tablespoon finely chopped
fresh oregano

1 tablespoon finely chopped
fresh tarragon

4 salmon fillets (6 ounces each)

Sorrel Cream

½ cup chopped fresh sorrel

¼ cup white wine

1 tablespoon chopped shallots

2 cups heavy cream

Salt and pepper

Baked Salmon in Pecan-Herb Crust with Sorrel Cream

TO PREPARE SALMON: Preheat oven to 350°F. In a small bowl, combine pecans, butter, basil, oregano, and tarragon; blend well. Spread mixture evenly over salmon fillets. Place fillets on a baking sheet and bake at 350°F for 20 minutes or until fish is firm.

TO PREPARE SORREL CREAM: In a saucepan, combine sorrel, wine, and shallots. Cook over medium heat for about 3 minutes or until mixture is almost dry. Add cream and mix well. Season with salt and pepper. Bring to a boil, then transfer to a blender. Purée until sauce is smooth.

To serve, spoon sauce on each plate, then place salmon on sauce.

Yield: 4 servings

CELEBRATING THE CLASSICS
MARÍA'S NEW MEXICAN KITCHEN

In 1950, a young homemaker named María, married to politician Gilbert López, began selling takeout food she prepared in her home kitchen. Over the years, María López enlarged a secondhand building by adding a covered patio and booths for her customers, who craved her traditional northern New Mexico food. Al Lucero and his wife, Laurie, bought the restaurant in 1985 and began making changes of their own, first putting Mexican fajitas on the menu and then adding hand-shaken, premium margaritas. (The restaurant's bar now offers more than one hundred variations of margaritas.) Lucero is outspoken about the authenticity of his New Mexican entrées, which are based on recipes his mother used when Al was growing up in Santa Fe.

Carne Adovada

TO PREPARE RED CHILE MARINADE: Place dried chile pods in a bowl and cover with hot water; let soak for about 20 minutes or until chiles are soft. Drain chiles and discard water. Combine chiles, garlic, and salt in blender container or food processor; add just enough water to cover. Purée until smooth, adding more water or more chiles if needed to achieve desired thickness. Transfer puréed mixture to a saucepan and simmer for 20 to 30 minutes or until mixture thickens slightly. Remove from heat and set aside.

TO PREPARE MEAT: Preheat oven to 375°F. Trim fat from pork and cut meat into one-inch cubes. Place cubes of meat in a lightly oiled baking pan and bake, uncovered, at 375°F for 30 minutes, stirring occasionally. Remove pan from oven and add Red Chile Marinade, crushed chiles, garlic powder, and salt; stir to blend with pan juices. Return to oven and bake for 30 to 45 minutes or until pork is tender enough to cut with a fork. Serve with flour tortillas.

Red Chile Marinade

6 to 8 dried red chile pods

4 garlic cloves, minced

½ teaspoon salt

Meat

2 pounds pork
(rump or shoulder cut)

1 cup crushed red chiles
(seeds included, if available)

1 tablespoon garlic powder

1 teaspoon salt

6 flour tortillas

Yield: Serves 6

María's La Última Margarita

1 lemon or lime wedge

Kosher salt, if desired

1½ ounces (3 tablespoons) fresh lemon juice

1¼ ounces (2½ tablespoons) premium tequila (100% agave)

¾ ounce (1½ tablespoons) Cointreau or Triple Sec

2 cups cracked ice or small ice cubes

MOISTEN RIM of margarita glass with the lemon or lime wedge, then dip rim into salt, if desired. Set glass aside. Measure lemon juice, tequila, and Cointreau or Triple Sec into a 16-ounce shaker filled with ice. Secure top on shaker and shake by hand for 5 to 10 seconds. Pour into prepared glass and garnish with a wedge of lemon or lime.

Yield: 1 serving

Beyond Santa Fe

Day-trip destinations near Santa Fe are as varied as the landscape, ranging from skiing and hiking in the mountains to visiting artists' studios and observing ceremonial dances at nearby Indian pueblos.

Bandelier National Monument combines the splendor of the Jémez Mountains with the fascinating history of the Anasazi, prehistoric ancestors of Pueblo Indians now living along the Río Grande. Bandelier protects the long-abandoned ruins of Anasazi dwellings, storage rooms, and sacred chambers, many of which are carved directly into the soft volcanic cliffs of Frijoles Canyon.

The village of Chimayó is home to descendants of Spanish colonists who settled in the foothills of the Sangre de Cristo Mountains two centuries ago. This farming community is known for its colorful weavings (many studios and galleries are tucked beneath the tall cottonwood trees) and the diminutive Santuario de Chimayó, built in 1814. Thousands of pilgrims come each year to gather the allegedly healing earth at this Catholic shrine, which is known as the Lourdes of the Southwest.

Follow the High Road to Taos into the mountains beyond Chimayó to see some of New Mexico's most magnificent scenery while glimpsing Spanish-speaking villages that have changed little since their founding. Ranchos de Taos is dominated by the beautiful San Francisco de Asís church, one of the most photographed adobe buildings in the world. A few miles beyond is Taos, known for its Indian pueblo, its plaza-centered shopping district, and its devotion to the arts.

The Turquoise Trail passes by Cerrillos, a historic turquoise mining center now used as a filming location for Hollywood westerns. Nearby is the newly revived art colony of Madrid, a company-owned coal mining town during the early twentieth century.

A COUNTRY HACIENDA

GABRIEL'S

L ocated about ten miles north of the Santa Fe Plaza, Gabriel's serves foods of the Southwest and Old Mexico. The setting is a spectacular hacienda-style courtyard, filled with fountains and flower gardens. Gabriel's is known for its festive atmosphere and fresh ingredients, which include tortillas made while you watch. According to Chef Saul Padilla, the restaurant's most popular appetizer is its traditional Mexican guacamole, a rich and spicy avocado dipping sauce prepared at tableside in a Molcajete bowl. Only five minutes away is the Santa Fe Opera, a world-class summer festival founded in 1957 to showcase a combination of popular classics, seldom-heard masterpieces, and world premieres. The amphitheater's open sides and backless stage allow views of dramatic sunsets and shimmering stars.

Gabriel's Guacamole

PLACE AVOCADOS in a large bowl and mash until smooth (you may want to leave a few chunks for texture). Add chile pepper, tomato, and onion; mix well. Season with salt and pepper. Add cilantro, garlic, and lime or lemon juice, if desired; mix well. The guacamole is best when served at room temperature within 2 hours of preparation (see Note). Serve with tortilla chips.

Yield: 4 servings

Note: If the guacamole will not be served right away, squeeze additional lime or lemon juice over the top or place an avocado pit in the guacamole to discourage discoloration. Cover and refrigerate.

3 large ripe avocados, peeled and pitted

1 small fresh jalapeño chile pepper, stemmed, seeded, and minced

1 medium Roma tomato, peeled (if desired), seeded, and finely diced

⅓ medium yellow onion, finely diced

Salt and black pepper (optional)

2 to 3 sprigs fresh cilantro, finely chopped

2 garlic cloves, finely minced

Juice of 1 lime or 1 small lemon (about 1 to 2 tablespoons), optional

Tortilla chips

Pilgrim's Rest

Restaurante Rancho de Chimayó

Throughout most of its history, the village of Chimayó was a quiet farming community whose residents were praised for producing some of the sweetest apples and spiciest chile peppers in New Mexico. In recent years, many residents have abandoned their orchards and fields, preferring to commute to full-time jobs in nearby Española or Los Alamos. Members of the Jaramillo family decided to stay put, and they devoted their energies to their apple trees and chile patch. The family's nineteenth-century adobe farmhouse has been transformed into Restaurante Rancho de Chimayó, which serves authentic northern New Mexico cuisine based on family recipes and using locally grown ingredients. The old house has thick adobe walls and bark-stripped vigas (roof beams) as well as a terraced backyard patio where food is served al fresco during warm months.

Sopaipillas

2 cups flour

1½ teaspoons sugar

1 teaspoon baking powder

1 teaspoon salt

1½ teaspoons oil plus oil for deep-frying
(preferably canola, rice bran, or corn oil)

½ cup lukewarm water

¼ cup evaporated milk,
at room temperature

Honey

COMBINE FLOUR, sugar, baking powder, and salt; sift into a large mixing bowl. Add 1½ teaspoons oil and blend with your fingertips. Add water and evaporated milk; stir until mixture forms a sticky ball of dough. Turn out onto a lightly floured surface and knead vigorously for about 1 minute. The dough should be "earlobe soft" and no longer sticky. Cover dough with a damp cloth and let rest for 15 minutes.

Divide the dough into three equal portions and form into balls. Cover the balls of dough with a damp cloth and let rest for another 15 to 30 minutes. (The dough can be refrigerated at this point for up to 4 hours.) Roll out each ball of dough on a lightly floured surface, forming a circle or oval approximately ¼ inch thick. (To keep dough from becoming tough, roll it quickly and handle it as little as possible.) Trim off ragged edges and discard. Using a sharp knife, cut each circle of dough into four wedges, then cover with a damp cloth. (Do not stack wedges of dough on top of each other.)

Place a stack of several paper towels near the stove. Pour oil for deep-frying into a wok or high-sided, heavy skillet to a depth of two inches and heat to 400°F. (Use a cooking thermometer to check, and do not allow oil to exceed this temperature. If oil starts to smoke, there is a danger of fire.) One by one, carefully and gently drop wedges of dough into the hot oil. (Do not crowd too many pieces of dough into the wok or skillet; cook just three or four at a time.) The wedges will sink briefly, then balloon to the surface. Spoon oil over sopaipillas when they begin to float, and after the tops puff up, turn over with tongs to cook the other side. Cook until light golden brown. (The total cooking time should be about 20 to 30 seconds per side.) Remove from oil with tongs and drain on paper towels. (If sopaipillas darken before they are fully puffed, lower the temperature of the oil a few degrees before continuing.) Repeat process until all dough has been fried. Place sopaipillas in a napkin-lined basket and serve with honey.

Yield: 12 sopaipillas

Madrid's Watering Hole
The Mine Shaft Tavern

The village of Madrid—named after an early Spanish settler and locally pronounced MAD-rid—is nestled in the foothills of the Ortíz Mountains. Founded around 1870, Madrid thrived until the 1940s, when a downturn in coal mining doomed the town. (The community's other claim to fame was a display of Christmas lights so extensive that commercial airlines would sometimes divert their planes during the holiday season so passengers could glimpse the lights from above.) Madrid was put up for sale for $250,000 in 1954, but there were no takers. Since then, several hundred artists, entrepreneurs, and free spirits have purchased individual lots, repopulating the ghost town. The Mine Shaft Tavern has a friendly Old West ambience and a forty-foot-long standup bar, the longest in New Mexico.

Blue Cheese Tavern Burger

½ pound lean ground beef

1 heaping tablespoon crumbled
blue cheese

3 fresh tomato slices

1 red onion slice

2 leaves romaine lettuce

1 sesame seed bun or Kaiser roll
(lightly toasted, if desired)

Condiments: mustard, mayonnaise,
ketchup, and/or
green chiles

FORM GROUND BEEF into a patty and grill or broil over medium-high heat to desired doneness—about 5 minutes for medium-rare. Turn burger just once. Top with cheese after turning so cheese will soften while burger continues to cook. Place cooked burger on bun and top with tomato, onion, and lettuce. Serve immediately with condiments of your choice.

Yield: 1 serving

Sangre de Cristo Hiker's Picnic

Santa Fe is blessed with almost instant access to some of the most beautiful scenery in the West, crisscrossed by trails and backcountry roads. During summer and early fall, few experiences are as delightful as a picnic in the Sangre de Cristo Mountains, which embrace the northern and eastern flanks of the city. Getting into the woods is as easy as following Artist Road out of downtown Santa Fe for about seventeen miles and arriving at the Santa Fe Ski Area. You will pass through various types of forest vegetation and by numerous trailheads and picnic areas as you ascend from 7,000 to 10,500 feet in altitude. In September and October, the mountain aspen turn brilliant shades of yellow and orange, offset by the deep green of surrounding pine, fir, and spruce.

*4 green chile vegetarian tamales
(bring more if you have hearty eaters)*

1 loaf Nativo wheat bread

8 ounces garlic-flavored goat cheese

*Seasonal fruits such as locally grown
apricots, peaches, cherries, or apples*

1 bottle Gruet brut sparkling wine

Sangre de Cristo Hikers Picnic

PLACE ITEMS in suitable containers and store in a cooler or picnic hamper for a trip to the mountains. If you will be hiking beyond the roadside picnic area, divide food among hikers in day-packs. When you find a beautiful forest meadow, settle down with blanket, arranging all items within easy reach. (Don't forget plates, utensils, cups, and napkins.)

Yield: 4 servings

Shopping List:

- Green chile vegetarian tamales are available at Posa's El Merendero takeout restaurants and at grocery stores in Santa Fe.

- Made from northern New Mexico–grown wheat, Nativo wheat bread is available at Cloud Cliff Bakery and at grocery stores in Santa Fe.

- Garlic-flavored goat cheese is available at Sweetwoods Dairy, at grocery stores in Santa Fe, and at the Santa Fe Farmers Market (open Tuesdays and Saturdays, 7:30 A.M. to noon, late April through October).

- Seasonal fruits are also available at the Santa Fe Farmers Market and at local grocery stores from July through October.

- Gruet wines are available from New Mexico's Gruet Winery and at local grocery and liquor stores.

Santa Fe Historical Timeline

900–1400	Ancestors of modern Pueblo Indians live, hunt, and fish along the banks of the Santa Fe River, site of present-day Santa Fe.
1540	The first official Spanish expedition to New Mexico is led by Spanish explorer Francisco Vásquez de Coronado.
1598	Spanish explorer Juan de Oñate leads a group of 129 colonists to found the first European settlement in New Mexico, located about thirty-five miles north of present-day Santa Fe near San Juan Pueblo. Oñate becomes the first governor-general of New Mexico.
1607–10	La Villa Real de la Santa Fé (The Royal City of the Holy Faith) is founded by Spanish colonists, relocating from their first settlement. (Historians disagree on the exact date.)
1609	Don Pedro de Peralta becomes the second governor-general of New Mexico.
1610	Santa Fe becomes the permanent capital of New Mexico. Construction of the Palace of the Governors begins.
1610–80	New settlers from Spain continue to arrive in Santa Fe, missionaries work to convert the Indians, and the Spanish policy of a closed empire and restricted trade is observed.
1625	La Conquistadora, now the oldest carved Madonna in the Americas, is brought to Santa Fe from Mexico City by Fray Alonzo de Benavides. The wooden figure remains on display in St. Francis Cathedral.
1626	San Miguel Chapel, Santa Fe's oldest church, is first constructed. The original structure is burned during the Pueblo Indian Revolt in 1680; in 1710, the chapel is completely rebuilt. It later becomes part of St. Michael's College, now the College of Santa Fe.
1680	The Pueblo Indian Revolt leads to the sacking of Santa Fe and the withdrawal of all Spaniards to El Paso. Pueblo Indians occupy Santa Fe for the next twelve years.
1692	The reconquest of Santa Fe (and New Mexico) by Spanish conquistadors led by Don Diego de Vargas is accomplished with little bloodshed.

1712	New Mexico's governor signs a proclamation that establishes an annual commemoration of the reconquest of Santa Fe—Fiesta de Santa Fe—to be held in September henceforth. In 1926 the event is expanded to include a series of public celebrations.
1796	Sanctification of Santuario de Guadalupe, the oldest shrine in the United States dedicated to Mexico's Virgin of Guadalupe. The church also marks the terminus of El Camino Real, the main trail connecting Santa Fe and Mexico City.
1821	Spain grants Mexico its independence, and New Mexico becomes a part of the new Republic of Mexico.
1821–80	No longer under Spain's rule, New Mexico is freed from the Spanish policy of a closed empire and restricted trade. The Santa Fe Trail serves as the main overland trade route linking Santa Fe (via Colorado, Oklahoma, Kansas, and Missouri) with the eastern United States.
1846–48	The United States and Mexico engage in the Mexican War. In 1846, U.S. General Stephen Watts Kearney raises the Stars and Stripes above Santa Fe's Palace of the Governors.
1850	New Mexico officially becomes a U.S. territory.
1851	Santa Fe is named the capital of the Territory of New Mexico.
1862	Santa Fe is briefly occupied by the Confederate Army during the American Civil War. A decisive battle at nearby Glorieta Pass restores New Mexico to Federal control.
1869	Catholic Archbishop Jean-Baptiste Lamy lays the cornerstone for St. Francis Cathedral in downtown Santa Fe. The French Gothic–Romanesque cathedral is constructed around a small adobe church built more than 150 years earlier and which is incorporated into the cathedral as Sacrament Chapel.
1879	Susan Wallace, wife of territorial governor (and *Ben Hur* author) Lew Wallace, writes to her son: "We should have another war with Old Mexico to make her take back New Mexico." Her frustrated husband earlier declared: "All calculations based on experiences elsewhere fail in New Mexico."

1880	Regular railroad service arrives in Santa Fe via a spur that connects to the main line at the village of Lamy, seventeen miles southeast of the city. The same route continues to carry freight and passengers today.
1898	During the Spanish-American War, Santa Fe and nearby Las Vegas supply many of the troops for Teddy Roosevelt's famous Rough Riders unit.
1909	In preparation for its 300th anniversary, the Palace of the Governors is renovated and becomes a state museum, preserving artifacts from New Mexico's Spanish colonial era. Other similar projects signal the start of the modern historical preservation movement in Santa Fe.
1912	Statehood is granted on January 6, making New Mexico the forty-seventh member of the Union.
1917	Completion of the Museum of Fine Arts on Palace Avenue, incorporating elements of New Mexico's Spanish-Pueblo Revival style exhibit at the 1915 Panama-California Exposition in San Diego.
1926	The burning of a huge puppet, Zozobra (Spanish for "Old Man Gloom")—created by artist Will Shuster, dancer Jacques Cartier, and newspaper editor Dana Johnson—is added to the annual Fiestas de Santa Fe rituals. (The puppet has since grown to a height of more than fifty feet.) That same year, Spanish Market is created by the Spanish Colonial Arts Society to support a style of arts and crafts from the era in which New Mexico was a colony of Spain.
1927	The Indian Market is established by the Southwestern Association for Indian Arts as a celebration of traditional Native American arts and crafts.
1935	La Sociedad Folklorica is founded to support Spanish culture, language, and tradition in Santa Fe. Also, the first art gallery (now closed) opens on Canyon Road, which has since become the center of the Santa Fe arts community.
1940	Construction begins on Cristo Rey Church, one of the largest adobe structures in Santa Fe. Built in Spanish Colonial style, it houses a stone altar screen dating from 1760.
1942–45	Santa Fe is the transportation and administrative center for the secret Manhattan Project at nearby Los Alamos during World War II. The project culminates with the development of

powerful atomic bombs—the first detonated in New Mexico in July 1945 and two others dropped on Hiroshima and Nagasaki, Japan, in August 1945.

1957   The Santa Fe Opera is founded, with the first performances on an outdoor stage (since upgraded) north of the city. The venue offers spectacular views of the Jémez and Sangre de Cristo mountains.

1958   A restrictive historical architecture zoning ordinance is adopted that establishes precise guidelines for preservation (and promotion) of Santa Fe's distinctive Spanish-Pueblo Revival style building designs.

1966   The present state capitol (nicknamed the "Roundhouse" because of its circular shape) is built at the corner of Don Gaspar Street and Paseo de Peralta.

1970s   Santa Fe emerges as a major U.S. art center, expanding by the end of the century to nearly two hundred galleries (exhibiting everything from Native Alaskan walrus tusk carvings to Southwest bronze cowboy sculptures).

1981   *Esquire* magazine describes Santa Fe as "the place to be."

1985–present   Entertainment industry celebrities flock to Santa Fe, with many establishing part-time or full-time residences. The roster includes Shirley MacLaine, Gene Hackman, Randy Travis, Brian Dennehy, Oprah Winfrey, James Taylor, Ali McGraw, Val Kilmer, Robert Redford, and Carol Burnett.

1990   For the first time in Santa Fe's history, Hispanics no longer represent a majority of the population. Collectively, Anglos, Asians, Native Americans, and African-Americans outnumber Hispanics by a small margin.

1992   In a survey of *Condé Nast Traveler* magazine readers, Santa Fe is named their favorite travel destination in the world.

2000   Santa Fe's estimated population reaches seventy thousand.

Annual Events in the Santa Fe Area

January Ceremonial dances at many Indian pueblos (Jan. 1 and Jan. 6) / Souper Bowl with local restaurants in charity competition for best soups (Saturday before Super Bowl) / Mark West Memorial Ski Team Fun Race at the Santa Fe Ski Area (date varies)

February Public trails open for cross-country skiing in nearby mountains / Ben and Pat Abruzzo Memorial Ski Team Race at the Santa Fe Ski Area (date varies)

March–April Good Friday pilgrimage to Santuario de Chimayó / Good Friday and Easter celebrations / Corn dances at the Santo Domingo Pueblo (Easter Sunday through following Wednesday)

April Closing day Surf 'n Ski celebration at Santa Fe Ski Area (usually second weekend) / Annual public cleaning of the Acequia Madre and other community-owned irrigation ditches (Saturday; date varies) / Santa Fe Farmers Market opens (opening date varies; through October)

May Taste of Santa Fe chefs competition (first weekend) / Cinco de Mayo commemorates Mexico's defeat of French forces in the nineteenth century (May 5) / Community Days on the Plaza (third weekend) / El Dorado Arts and Crafts Studio Tour (third weekend) / Santa Fe Century Bike Ride (date varies) / Whitewater rafting season begins in canyons of the nearby Río Grande (through mid-October)

June Spring Festival at El Rancho de las Golondrinas, a living history museum of New Mexico history, culture, and architecture, in La Cienega (first weekend) / Santa Fe Arts and Crafts Festival on the Plaza (third weekend) / Rodeo de Santa Fe (fourth weekend)

late June–early July Summer performing arts season begins, including performances by María Benítez Teatro Flamenco, Santa Fe Chamber Music Festival, Santa Fe Desert Chorale, Santa Fe Opera, Santa Fe Stages, and Shakespeare in Santa Fe

July Wine Festival at El Rancho de las Golondrinas (first weekend) / Pancake Breakfast on the Plaza (July 4) / Nambé Falls Celebration at the Nambé Pueblo (July 4) / Spanish Market on the Plaza (last weekend)

August Summer Festival at El Rancho de las Golondrinas (first weekend) / Mountain Man Rendezvous and Trade Fair at the Palace of the Governors (first or second weekend) / Santa Fe County Fair at the Rodeo Grounds (second weekend) / Indian Market on the Plaza (third weekend)

September Fiestas de Santa Fe (first weekend after Labor Day, beginning with burning of Zozobra on Thursday night; later events include a grand ball, pet parade, and candlelight religious processions) / Wine and Chile Fiesta (last weekend)

October Aspen leaves turn bright orange and yellow in the Santa Fe National Forest overlooking Santa Fe / Harvest Festival at El Rancho de las Golondrinas (first weekend) / International Balloon Fiesta in Albuquerque (first through second weekend) / Mystery Train Rides on the Santa Fe Southern Railway (Oct. 31)

November Feast of San Diego at the Tesuque Pueblo (Nov. 12) / Santa Fe Ski Area opens (usually the day after Thanksgiving, depending on snow conditions) / Santa Fe Film Festival (last Wednesday through following weekend)

December Winter Spanish Market (first weekend) / Christmas Open House at Madrid (first and second weekends) / Christmas-related events

include Las Posadas procession, farolito and luminaria walks, Our Lady of Guadalupe ceremonies, Christmas at the Palace of the Governors events, concerts, and dances at various Indian pueblos (Dec. 24 and 25 as well as other dates throughout the month)

For more information about these and other events in Santa Fe, contact:

Santa Fe Convention & Visitors Bureau
P.O. Box 909
Santa Fe, NM 87504-0000
Phone 505.984.6760 or 800.777.2480
Web site www.santafe.org
E-mail santafe@santafe.org

Index